100 STRATEGIES OF WAR

百戰奇法

ASIAPAC COMIC SERIES
STRATEGY & LEADERSHIP

Brilliant Tactics in Action

100 STRATEGIES OF WAR
百戰奇法

WANG XUANMING

Translated by
Yeo Ai Hoon

ASIAPAC • SINGAPORE

Publisher
ASIAPAC BOOKS PTE LTD
629 Aljunied Road #04-06
Cititech Industrial Building
Singapore 1438
Tel: 7453868
Fax: 7453822

First published December 1993
Reprinted April 1994

© ASIAPAC BOOKS, 1993
ISBN 981-3029-16-1

All rights reserved. No part of this publication may be reproduced, stored in a retrieval system, or transmitted, in any form or by any means electronic, mechanical, photocopying, recording, or otherwise, without the prior written permission of the publisher.
If this copy is defective, kindly exchange it at the above address.

Cover design by Bay Song Lin
Typeset by Quaser Technology Pte Ltd
Body text in 8/9 pt Helvetica
Printed in Singapore by
Loi Printing Pte Ltd

Publisher's Note

100 Strategies of War is a valuable book which incorporates the various strategies used in historical Chinese battles. These strategies are still applicable in today's modern warfare.

We are pleased to present the work of Wang Xuanming, a contemporary cartoonist from Mainland China, who has illustrated a series of ancient Chinese military classics into comics. The first four books, *Thirty-six Stratagems, Six Strategies for War, Gems of Chinese Wisdom* and *Three Strategies of Huang Shi Gong* have been warmly received by our readers. *100 Strategies of War* is the fifth book in this series.

We feel honoured to have the cartoonist, Wang Xuanming's permission to the translation rights to his best-selling comics. We would also like to thank Ms Yeo Ai Hoon for translating this volume, Mr Chiang Ming Yu for his review, and the production team for putting in their best effort in the publication of this series.

Titles in the Strategy and Leadership series:

The Art of War: Chinese Military Classic
Thirty-six Stratagems: Secret Art of War
Six Strategies for War: The Practice of Effective Leadership
Gems of Chinese Wisdom: Mastering the Art of Leadership
Three Strategies of Huang Shi Gong: The Art of Government
100 Strategies of War: Brilliant Tactics in Action

100 Strategies of War is the last book in the series of adaptations of ancient Chinese military classics by cartoonist Wang Xuanming. The original Chinese classic was itself based on twenty-one historical books which recorded the battles fought over a period of no less than 1,600 years in China's history.

Just as anyone should sip Chinese tea, the reader must digest the contents slowly, savouring every lesson or "strategy". Because of the sheer number of lessons to be found here, one should not expect to finish this book in one sitting. Each lesson, or "strategy", presented succinctly in the form of an elaboration of the strategy, contains a short "rule" summarizing it, and is completed by a historical illustration. This represents a departure from the style of the earlier books on strategy in the same series. It is also an exhaustive volume on military strategies which demonstrates many brilliant tactics in action.

The underlying principles of these strategies are applicable to modern warfare. Special emphasis is placed on morale, intelligence, logistics and the use of terrain. In particular, I am impressed by the ability of Generals Han Xin and Huang Fusong who used the natural elements to aid them in battle.

I am gratified to be able to review the titles under the Leadership & Strategy Series by Wang Xuanming, to whom I offer many thanks for the enjoyment he has given. I hope that you, the reader, will also gain much knowledge and pleasure from this book.

Chiang Ming Yu
Chairman, Wargame Club
Singapore Armed Forces Reservists' Association

About the Editor/Illustrator

Wang Xuanming, a contemporary cartoonist in China, was born in Beijing in 1950. He was trained formally in commercial art and industrial art. Since 1972, he has been engaged in various aspects of artistic work, even undertaking the production of screen advertisements and artistic stage designs. Wang's contribution to the field of art is immense. He frequently explores various ways of expressing his artistic talents. Besides a lot of cartoons, picture books, and illustrations, he also does oil paintings and posters. His works have on many occasions entered nationwide art exhibitions, won awards in several art competitions, and have been selected for inclusion in various art albums.

Wang's cartoons, illustrations, and other works have been serialized in all the major newspapers and publications in Beijing since 1980. His cartoons entitled *Different Gravitational Force* is praised by famous Chinese artists, and was selected for inclusion in the *Anthology of Chinese Scientific Cartoons*. In 1987, he participated in the creation of the animated cartoon *Brother Elephant*, which captured the hearts of many children when it was first shown on television.

Wang has worked with many publishers in Beijing, such as China Friendly Publishing Co., Chinese Cultural Publishing Co., Huaxia Publishing Co., People's Art Publishing Co., and Zhaohua Publishing Co. He has gained the trust and confidence of both publishers and artists alike.

In his latest comic series, *Books of Strategy*, he uses a simple and humorous art form to introduce ancient Chinese military classics to modern readers. The books were very well received by people from all walks of life when they were first published in China; the Beijing Radio Station made a special interview of this series of books and highly recommended it to the public. This series is published by China Friendly Publishing Co. in China, and by Treasure Creation Co. Ltd. in Hongkong. Asiapac Books in Singapore is the publisher for the English edition of this series.

Wang is at present an art editor at the *China Science and Technology Daily*.

Preface

Books on the art of war occupy an important place in traditional Chinese culture. Their vast scale, rich content, extensive and profound philosophy are highly acclaimed. Military thinking not only sums up and guides the thousands of earthshaking wars in the history of China, but has also influenced the development of Chinese military affairs, philosophy, literature and technology.

Amongst the many ancient books on military affairs, *100 Strategies of War* is an outstanding example. Its most distinguishing feature is that it ingeniously combines military teachings with historical events, using examples of various famous battles to illustrate abstract military principles. The entire book records 99 famous battles spanning 1,645 years from the Spring and Autumn Period to the Five Dynasties. Of these, 19 are from the Spring and Autumn Period, 33 from the Qin and Han Period, 10 from the Three Kingdoms Period, 19 from the Wei, Jin, Northern and Southern Dynasties; and 18 from the Sui and Tang Dynasties. These examples are culled from 21 historical books and classified according to the unique military characteristics of each battle. Hence, this book makes for convincing and interesting reading.

This selection of a hundred strategies of war pays particular attention to those battles that are large-scale, unique and of great impact. These include the Battles of Changshao and Chengpu during the Spring and Autumn Period, the Batttles of Maling and Jimo during the Warring States Period, the Battle between Chu and Han towards the end of the Qin Dynasty, the Battle of Guandu towards the end of the Han Dynasty, the Battle of Fei River during the Eastern and Western Jin Dynasties, and the Battles of Luoyang and Cai city during the Tang Dynasty. These battles have provided much valuable experience for later generations to ponder on and draw lessons from. Because *100 Strategies of War* combines historical wars with military teachings, it gives readers a fresh angle to studying history and battles.

100 Strategies of War was written during the Song Dynasty, a few years later than Sun Zi's *Art of War*. The author used Sun Zi's thoughts as a foundation and at the same time developed new ideas. Therefore, the views of this book are more comprehensive and profound.

In discussing the many aspects of military affairs, *100 Strategies of War* always looks at the two sides of a situation and explores various angles before developing them into scientific rules. Full of philosophical thinking, this book motivates readers to delve into the various strategies. According to the book, opposites such as attack and defence, safety and danger, victory and defeat, life and death, will interchange under certain conditions. If those who are victorious become complacent because of their victory, they will face defeat eventually. If one is fearful of death and retreats under a critical situation, he will be killed instead. These military thoughts are simple but are highly regarded by military strategists.

In the ever-changing world of today, people are faced with many more new challenges. If you can be well-versed with the thoughts contained in this book, it will increase your ability to respond to various situations in life so that you can be victorious in your life and undertakings.

Wang Xuanming

Contents

Volume 1 .... 3 – 32

Strategy 1	Knowing One's Enemy Well before a Battle	计战
Strategy 2	Foiling the Enemy's Plan	谋战
Strategy 3	Using Espionage	间战
Strategy 4	Using Elite Troops as the Vanguard	选战
Strategy 5	Deployment of Foot Soldiers	步战
Strategy 6	Deployment of Horsemen	骑战
Strategy 7	Fighting a Sea Battle	舟战
Strategy 8	Using Chariots	车战
Strategy 9	Soldiers' Trust in the Commander	信战
Strategy 10	Training of Soldiers	教战

Volume 2 .... 33 – 52

Strategy 11	Fighting when One's Forces Outnumber the Enemy's	众战
Strategy 12	Fighting when One's Forces are Outnumbered	寡战
Strategy 13	Treating One's Soldiers Well	爱战
Strategy 14	Instilling in Soldiers a Sense of Awe and Respect for the General	威战
Strategy 15	Using Incentives	赏战
Strategy 16	Using Punishment	罚战
Strategy 17	Fighting on Home Ground	主战
Strategy 18	Fighting on Enemy Ground	客战
Strategy 19	Fighting when One's Army is Strong	强战
Strategy 20	Fighting when One's Army is Weaker	弱战

Volume 3 .... 53 – 67

Strategy 21	Making the Enemy feel Arrogant	骄战
Strategy 22	Forming Alliance with Neighbouring States	交战
Strategy 23	Putting up False Appearances	形战
Strategy 24	Seizing the Opportunity to Attack	势战
Strategy 25	Fighting during the Day	昼战
Strategy 26	Fighting at Night	夜战
Strategy 27	Being Prepared and on the Alert during an Expedition	备战
Strategy 28	Ensuring Sufficient Food Supply	粮战
Strategy 29	Using Local Guides	导战
Strategy 30	Understanding the Battleground Well	知战

Volume 4 .... 68 – 84
Strategy 31	Using Reconnaissance	斥战
Strategy 32	Fighting in Marshes	泽战
Strategy 33	Fighting for a Strategic Location	争战
Strategy 34	Occupying an Advantageous Location	地战
Strategy 35	Fighting in the Mountains	山战
Strategy 36	Fighting in the Valley	谷战
Strategy 37	Being on the Offensive	攻战
Strategy 38	Being on the Defensive	守战
Strategy 39	Being the First to Attack	先战
Strategy 40	Biding for Time in Battle	后战

Volume 5 .... 85 – 101
Strategy 41	Launching a Surprise Attack	奇战
Strategy 42	Fighting a Direct Battle	正战
Strategy 43	Using Illusion	虚战
Strategy 44	Being on Guard against a Strong Enemy	实战
Strategy 45	Understanding the Enemy Situation	轻战
Strategy 46	Being Cautious in a Battle	重战
Strategy 47	Using Small Gains to Entice the Enemy	利战
Strategy 48	Setting up Barriers along Strategic Locations	害战
Strategy 49	Being Calm in a Battle	安战
Strategy 50	Fighting in a Dangerous Situation	危战

Volume 6 .... 102 – 122
Strategy 51	Fighting in a Desperate Situation	死战
Strategy 52	Fighting Courageously	生战
Strategy 53	Pillaging the Enemy's Food Supply	饥战
Strategy 54	Fighting when the Enemy Forces Face a Food Shortage	饱战
Strategy 55	Avoiding a Battle when One's Troops Arrive Late and are Tired	劳战
Strategy 56	Being Alert, not Complacent after a Victory	佚战
Strategy 57	Being Prepared Despite a Victory	胜战
Strategy 58	Dealing with Defeat	败战
Strategy 59	Launching a Quick Attack	进战
Strategy 60	Withdrawing when Outnumbered	退战

Volume 7 .... 123 – 148
Strategy 61	Fighting a Provocative Battle	挑战
Strategy 62	Gaining the Initiative to Fight	致战

Strategy 63	Fighting from Afar	远战
Strategy 64	Fighting from Near	近战
Strategy 65	Fighting Near a River	水战
Strategy 66	Launching a Fire Attack	火战
Strategy 67	Besieging a City	缓战
Strategy 68	Fighting a Quick Battle	速战
Strategy 69	Fighting a Well-prepared Enemy	整战
Strategy 70	Fighting a Confused Enemy	乱战

Volume 8 .... 149 – 168

Strategy 71	Division of One's Troops	分战
Strategy 72	Consolidating One's Forces in Battle	合战
Strategy 73	Instilling Hatred Against the Enemy Within One's Troops	怒战
Strategy 74	Boosting the Soldiers' Morale	气战
Strategy 75	Pursuing the Enemy	逐战
Strategy 76	Fighting a Retreating Enemy	归战
Strategy 77	Taking the Initiative Not to Fight	不战
Strategy 78	Forcing the Defending Enemy to Fight	必战
Strategy 79	Avoid Engaging an Enemy with High Morale	避战
Strategy 80	Laying a Siege	围战

Volume 9 .... 169 – 184

Strategy 81	Causing the Enemy to be Defenceless	声战
Strategy 82	Using Peace Talks as a Means to Launch a Surprise Attack	和战
Strategy 83	Making Careful Observations of the Enemy instead of Fleeing	受战
Strategy 84	Being Cautious when the Enemy Forces Surrender	降战
Strategy 85	Choosing the Right Time to Fight	天战
Strategy 86	Maintaining Calm and Stability within One's Troops	人战
Strategy 87	Being Loyal to One's Troops in Times of Danger	难战
Strategy 88	Attacking the Area that is Easiest to Conquer	易战
Strategy 89	Sowing Discord in the Enemy Camp	离战
Strategy 90	Using Baits to Entice the Enemy	饵战

Volume 10 .... 185 – 200

Strategy 91	Misleading the Enemy	疑战
Strategy 92	Fighting a Fleeing Enemy	穷战
Strategy 93	Taking Advantage of Wind Conditions In Battle	风战

Strategy 94	Taking Advantage of a Snowy Condition to Launch an Attack	雪战
Strategy 95	Building up One's Forces for Battle	养战
Strategy 96	Getting Rid of Cowardly Soldiers and Deserters, Calming Soldiers' Fears	畏战
Strategy 97	Severing Communication Between One's Soldiers and their Families	书战
Strategy 98	Being Flexible Enough to Adopt a Strategy According to the Situation	变战
Strategy 99	Fighting a Justifiable Battle	好战
Strategy 100	Combat Readiness during Peacetime	忘战

百戰奇法

100 Strategies of War

Volume 1

Strategy 1 – Knowing One's Enemy Well before a Battle

In any battle, detailed planning is of foremost importance. Before engaging in any battle, estimate the ability of one's generals, the strength of one's enemies, the consideration of locations as well as the sufficiency of supplies. Launch an attack only after careful consideration and planning.

Rule: Know one's enemies and plan for dangers that may occur from far and near.

Strategy 2 — Foiling the Enemy's Plan

Oppose the enemy's plan with a strategy and they will knuckle under you.

Rule: Formulate a strategy before going on an expedition.

Strategy 3 — Using Espionage

Before sending an expedition, make use of espionage to gather information about the enemy's activities, numerical strength, capability, troops, supplies, etc.

Rule: There is no place where espionage can't be used.

Strategy 4 — Using Elite Troops as the Vanguard

To be victorious in battle, select courageous generals and soldiers to be the vanguard. On the one hand, this will boost the soldiers' morale; on the other hand, it will deflate the enemy's might.

Rule: An army without a vanguard will be defeated.

Strategy 5 — Deployment of Foot Soldiers

When your foot soldiers engage the enemy's horsemen, select hills or dangerous paths as your battleground. If these are not available, construct barricades or use tripping wires to hinder the enemy troops' movements.

When fighting on level ground, shield the soldiers with chariots. Divide the forces to launch attacks and be on the defensive as well. When attacked from one side, protect the troops from both sides; if attacked from two sides, split the army to harass the enemy from behind; if attacked from four sides, form a circle and fight from all sides. Let the horsemen pursue the enemy while the foot soldiers follow behind.

Rule: Foot soldiers and horsemen should stick to dangerous paths and hills.

Strategy 6 — Deployment of Horsemen

Strategy 7 — Fighting a Sea Battle

When fighting with the enemy across rivers, boats are necessary. Always occupy the upstream and make sure that the wind is behind you. One will also be able to make use of fire as a means of attack.

Rule: To ensure success, do not go against the current.

One has to depend on boats when fighting with the enemy on water. Select a position where both the current and wind directions are favourable.

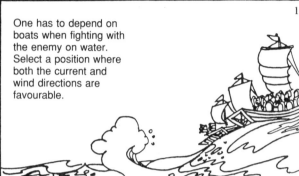

When the wind direction is favourable, make use of fire to destroy the enemy.

In an upstream position, one can use boats to attack the enemy downstream.

During the Spring and Autumn Period, Prince Guang of Wu led an army to attack Chu. Both armies were locked in a stalemate at the banks of Zhangan.

Strategy 8 — Using Chariots

When fighting with foot soldiers and horsemen in the plains, make use of chariots to achieve victory. This helps the troops to consolidate their strength, act as a shield and also help discipline the troops.

Rule: Use chariots in wide plains.

1. When fighting with the enemy foot soldiers and horsemen in the plains, use chariots as a form of defence.

2. There are three benefits. Firstly, it boosts the morale of the troops; secondly it blocks the enemy's attacks and thirdly, it ensures discipline of the troops.

3. During the Western Jin era, General Ma Long led an army to attack the Qiang tribal army.

"Recruit skilled archers who know how to use strong bows."

4. After careful selection, 3,500 archers were recruited.

5. After crossing the Wen River, the Jin soldiers met the Qiang army.

Strategy 9 — Soldiers' Trust in the Commander

When fighting, soldiers must be prepared to die without fear or regret. If the top echelon can be trusted, the soldiers will give of their best without questioning.

Rule: If the commander is trustworthy, the soldiers will have no hesitation in following his orders.

Strategy 10 — Training of Soldiers

Volume 2

Strategy 11 — Fighting when One's Forces Outnumber the Enemy's

Whenever one outnumbers the enemies considerably, do not fight in narrow dangerous paths but in wide plains. The troops must also know when to advance and retreat.

Rule: To gain victory, let one's troops know when to advance and retreat.

33

Strategy 12 — Fighting when One's Forces are Outnumbered

If one is outnumbered by the enemies, fight during dusk and wait in ambush behind thick growths of grass or narrow paths.

Rule: Fight in narrow paths when outnumbered.

Strategy 13 — Treating One's Soldiers Well

Soldiers who are well-treated by their commander would rather sacrifice their lives than retreat. They will look up to the commander who treats them well. During times of peril, they will be willing to lay down their lives.

Rule: Treat the soldiers like your own kith and kin; and they will be willing to fight to the death.

Strategy 14 — Instilling in Soldiers a Sense of Awe and Respect for the General

If soldiers dare to move ahead but dare not retreat, it is because they fear the general and not the enemy. Those who retreat but dare not proceed are afraid of the enemy. Soldiers who obey orders despite danger do so because they are in awe of the general due to his strictness.

Rule: Dignity and strict discipline overrides benevolence.

Strategy 15 — Using Incentives

Although faced with high city fortifications and heavy archery volleys, soldiers are prepared to rush into battle because they are offered attractive incentives.

Rule: Attractive incentives will motivate one's soldiers to brave dangers.

Strategy 16 — Using Punishment

To ensure that soldiers fight on and do not retreat, punish severely those who retreat easily.

Rule: Immediate punishment without exception instils discipline.

Strategy 17 — Fighting on Home Ground

Never take it lightly when you are fighting in your own territory as the soldiers are concerned about their families. Gather the people and protect the city to prepare for any dangers. Cut off the supply routes of the enemy. When the enemy cannot find any opportunity to fight and as their own supplies diminish, they will be tired and trapped.

Rule: To fight within one's home territory puts one on the intiative, enabling one to become the host of the battle.

Strategy 18 — Fighting on Enemy Ground

During a war, the army should penetrate deep into the enemy's territory.

Rule: Fighting deep within the enemy territory will enable one to regain the initiative.

Strategy 19 — Fighting when One's Army is Strong

Although one may have a stronger, bigger army, one can give the enemy the impression that one's forces are weak. When attacked, elite troops can be deployed to counter-attack the enemy.

Rule: Don't show your real strength. Feign incapability.

During the Warring States Period, Zhao general, Li Mu guarded Yanmen.

Strategy 20 — Fighting when One's Army is Weaker

If one is outnumbered by a stronger enemy, put up more banners and make more fire stoves to give the enemy the impression that one has a huge army. They will not be able to gauge one's actual military strength and the troops can then make a safe retreat.

Rule: The strengths and weaknesses of one's army can be feigned.

1. The enemy is stronger and has more soldiers, how should we fight?

2. Get the people to prepare more banners and everyone is to build more stoves.

3. They have stoves that can cook food for 100,000 soldiers!

4. When the enemy is undecided, we can safely disperse. Fight! Don't fight!

By increasing the number of stoves, Han general, Yuyu successfully overcame the blockade put up by the Jiang Hu soldiers. Those who use the right strategies wisely in unfavourable circumstances will escape from difficulties and turn the table on the enemy.

Volume 3

Strategy 21 — Making the Enemy Feel Arrogant

If the enemy is strong, one may not be able to win the war.

In this instance, it is wise to be modest when dealing with them. At the same time, offer them handsome gifts to flatter them and wait for an opportunity to attack.

Rule: Humility enables one to achieve victory.

Strategy 22 — Forming Alliance with Neighbouring States

When engaged in a war, one should not forget the importance of maintaining good diplomatic relations with neighbouring countries. By being diplomatic and humble towards them, and by offering them generous bribes to gain their support, will stand one in good stead.

Rule: When fighting in an advanced country, it is good to build up diplomatic relations with the enemy's neighbouring states.

1 When fighting with the enemy, form alliances with the enemy's neighbours.

Thank you for your support.

2 When one attacks the enemy from the front, one's allies will be able to impede the enemy from behind.

3 Attack the enemy from both the front and back so that they are trapped.

4 During the Three Kingdoms Period, Shu general, Guan Yu surrounded the city of Fan in Wei and captured General Yu Jin. This caused Cao Cao to be very nervous.

About 30,000 men and horses have been captured.

5 Guan Yu has made a formidable move. It looks like we have to forsake Xuchang and move the capital to the river north to avoid conflicts.

Strategy 23 — Putting Up False Appearances

When one is outnumbered, one should create an illusion to weaken the enemy's dominant position. Once distracted, the enemy will have to deploy their troops to be on guard. One can then assemble the forces to launch an attack.

Rule: Make the enemy think that one is superior to them to expose their weak points, while concealing one's real situation.

Strategy 24 — Seizing the Opportunity to Attack

Opportunists are those who know how to take advantage of a situation. Whenever the enemy troops face an adverse situation, one should seize the opportunity to fight back.

Rule: Take advantage of the situation to render the enemy ineffective.

Strategy 25 — Fighting during the Day

During day battles, put up more banners to confuse the enemy into thinking that one has a large number of troops.

Rule: Put up more banners during day battles.

Strategy 26 — Fighting at Night

When fighting at night, make good use of drums and fire to undermine the enemy's ability to see and hear, causing them to be confused, not knowing which strategy to adopt.

Rule: Make use of drums and fire during a night battle.

Strategy 27 — Being Prepared and on the Alert during an Expedition

On an expedition, guard against being intercepted while on the move, being ambushed while resting, being attacked by fire on a windy day; and beware of thefts by the enemy.

Rule: Be well prepared for a battle.

Strategy 28 — Ensuring Sufficient Food Supply

In a stalemate, the army that has food supplies will win. Safeguard your food supplies to prevent them from being plundered. Deploy elite troops to cut off the enemy's supply route. Without food, they will have to disperse and this will be an opportune time to attack them.

Rule: An army that has no adequate food supplies will eventually be destroyed.

1 It is difficult to predict victory and defeat in a stalemate.

2 Whoever has sufficient food supplies will be able to persevere to the end and win.

5 Guard your own food supplies carefully and ensure its smooth flow.

4 Send a small troop of elite soldiers to plunder the enemy's food supplies.

3 Towards the end of the Han dynasty, Cao Cao burnt the food supplies of Yuan Shao and achieved victory even though Yuan Shao had superior troops.

How can we fight on a hungry stomach? We'd better go home.

Having sufficient food supplies is an important material foundation in a war. Without the safeguard of food supplies, a war cannot be fought. Similarly, you need the security of material things in any undertakings.

Strategy 29 — Using Local Guides

When fighting, use the local people as guides to understand the terrain and roads.

Rule: Those who do not use local guides will not have the advantage of favourable geographical positions.

Strategy 30 — Understanding the Battleground Well

When sending soldiers on a war expedition, one needs to understand the battleground beforehand. If one can make the enemy come as planned, one will win. Knowing the battleground and when the battle will take place enables one to make adequate preparations.

Rule: If one has prior knowledge of the battleground and the date of battle, one can fight well even in a place far from home.

Volume 4

Strategy 31 — Using Reconnaissance

When troops are on the move, one must first make a reconnaissance of enemy territories. Form groups and everyone is to hold a flag and take turns to be on guard. Step up reconnaissance of enemy troops along the way. Once they are spotted, report to the commander-in-chief immediately.

Rule: He who is well prepared to seize opportunities in a battle will win.

Strategy 32 — Fighting in Marshes

Soldiers on a war expedition may come across marshlands or low-lying areas, but do not station troops there. If necessary, encamp on highlands. Stay where there are reeds against a clump of trees. This will enable troops to be on guard against floods and at the same time, be on the alert for enemy troops.

Rule: It is best to cross the marshes as soon as possible and to stay on higher grounds.

Strategy 33 — Fighting for a Strategic Location

It is important to gain a foothold of strategic terrain during a battle. If the enemy forces have already occupied it, one should not attack them. Instead, wait for an opportune time before launching an attack.

Rule: If the enemy troops have already seized control of a keyground, do not attack them.

Strategy 34 — Occupying an Advantageous Location

When fighting, the army must occupy an advantageous location so that even though small in number, one can still defeat the enemy. If one knows the enemy's weakness without occupying an advantageous position, only half the battle is won.

Rule: An advantageous location is better than good timing.

Strategy 35 — Fighting in the Mountains

Whether fighting in the jungle or flat plains, one must occupy the higher grounds. This is an advantageous position for launching attacks.

Rule: When fighting a battle in the mountains, it is to one's advantage to charge from the higher ground.

Strategy 36 — Fighting in the Valley

When leading troops across dangerous paths, one has to rely on the valleys. On the one hand, the troops have easy access to water and grasslands. On the other hand, they can rely on the rugged terrain for protection.

Rule: Marching troops should stay close to the valleys when passing through mountains.

Strategy 37 — Being on the Offensive

Understand the enemy's position well before mounting an offensive to ensure victory.

Rule: If there is a possibility of winning a resounding victory, one should be on the offensive.

Strategy 38 — Being on the Defensive

Knowing that there is no chance of victory, one should adopt a defensive strategy.

Rule: If one cannot win the battle, one must be on the defensive.

Our army does not have the ability to defeat the enemy yet, what strategy should we adopt?

Since our forces are inadequate, we should be on the defensive.

When the enemy's forces are tired, we can launch a surprise attack and achieve victory.

In suppressing the rebellion of the seven commanderies of Chu and Wu, Western Han general, Zhou Yafu persisted in defending the city and foiled the enemy's war plans, achieving victory as a result.

Emperor Wu, I've got bad news. Zhou Yafu has sent people to cut off our food supply route.

Because the Han army adopted the right strategy, the rebel armies were soon suppressed, as they became tired and their food supply depleted.

Strategy 39 — Being the First to Attack

When the enemy troops do not have a proper formation, grasp hold of the opportunity to attack them first. Victory is assured, as the confidence and morale of the enemy will be shaken.

Rule: To win a battle, be the first to attack.

Strategy 40 — Biding for Time in Battle

If the enemy troops are strong and their morale is high, it is not time to fight yet. The right time to fight is when they are not quite stabilised and their morale is low.

Rule: Bide for time – Wait till the enemy's morale is weakened before attacking them.

Volume 5

Strategy 41 — Launching a Surprise Attack

A surprise attack catches the enemy off guard. It means attacking the enemy forces when and where they least expect it. In this way, they do not know where to put up their defence.

Rule: Where the enemy forces are weakly defended, an attack on them will enable one to achieve victory.

* 1 li is equivalent to ½ km.

Strategy 42 — Fighting a Direct Battle

When the road is not passable during a battle, food supplies cannot be delivered; and ploy and bribery cannot work, one has to engage in a frontal attack. To do so, one must deploy a highly combative army equipped with good weapons. The general has to make clear to his soldiers the system of reward and punishment, and ensure that commands are followed.

Rule: Without the use of frontal attacks, one cannot go on a long war expedition.

Strategy 43 — Using Illusion

When one's forces are much weaker than the enemy's, one should give them the impression of having a formidable force, so that they will not dare pick a fight.

Rule: When the enemy forces do not dare to fight, it is because one has tricked them into it.

Strategy 44 — Being on Guard against a Strong Enemy

When faced with a strong enemy, even more intense preparations must be made.

Rule: To face strong opponents, always be well prepared.

Strategy 45 — Understanding the Enemy Situation

In a battle, it is important to study the enemy's movements and situation carefully. It is not wise to fight a war blindly without a proper strategy, otherwise defeat is inevitable.

Rule: Courageous soldiers without a proper strategy will be defeated.

Strategy 46 — Being Cautious in a Battle

Fighting the enemy is a serious matter. Be well positioned to act against them at the right moment. Avoid conflict when in a disadvantageous position so as not to be trapped.

Rule: Troops that are not mobilized should be stable as the lofty mountains.

Strategy 47 — Using Small Gains to Entice the Enemy

If the enemy's generals are dull and cannot adapt to changes easily, use small gains to entice them. By offering them benefits, it lowers their defences and brings about complacency. The greedy enemy troops who are least prepared for war are vulnerable and this is the time to ambush them.

Rule: Make use of small gains to lure the enemy out of their strongholds.

Strategy 48 — Setting up Barriers along Strategic Locations

When guarding the border, to prevent the enemy from intruding into one's territory, lay some ambushes or construct barriers at strategic points. The enemy will not dare attack easily.

Rule: Create obstructions to ward off enemy intrusions.

Strategy 49 — Being Calm in a Battle

If the enemy troops that come from afar are full of fighting spirit and poised for a quick fight, maintain one's position. At the same time, build moats and ditches while waiting for the enemy to be weary. If they try to pick a fight, avoid them.

Rule: Steadiness brings peace.

Strategy 50 — Fighting in a Dangerous Situation

When placed in a dangerous position, one must encourage the soldiers to fight to the end.
Rule: Soldiers must not be afraid when faced with a critical situation.

Volume 6

Strategy 51 — Fighting in a Desperate Situation

If the enemy is strong and one's soldiers are uncertain and unwilling to fight with their lives, defeat is at hand. Make the soldiers realize that there is no other alternative except to fight for survival. Kill the cows, burn the provisions, destroy the boats to dash the soldiers' hopes of escaping with their lives.

Rule: The troops must fight with the courage of desperation to survive.

1. Make it clear to the soldiers that they are on 'Death Ground' and that the only way is for them to fight bravely.

2. When faced with a strong army, the troops may lose courage and confidence.

   Oh dear! It's terrifying!

3. Burn all food provisions and fill up the stoves.

4. Break the cauldrons and sink the boats to dash all hopes of escape.

5. The entire army must adopt the attitude of fighting to the death. The soldiers may well have a narrow escape.

Strategy 52 — Fighting Courageously

If the location is favourable, the troops are in position, the commands have been given, the surprise troops have been organised, one has to go all out to fight. If the general becomes cowardly at the last minute, the troops will be killed instead.

Rule: Those who are afraid to fight will die.

Strategy 53 — Pillaging the Enemy's Food Supply

When sending a punitive expedition into the enemy's territory, and faced with a lack of food supply, plunder the enemy's food provisions for one's own soldiers.

Rule: Steal the enemy's food supply for one's army.

Strategy 54 — Fighting when the Enemy Forces Face a Food Shortage

When the enemy forces come from afar and their food supply is insufficient, avoid fighting them. Wait till their food supply has run out before attacking them.

Rule: Fight the enemy when they have run out of food.

Strategy 55 — Avoiding a Battle when One's Troops Arrive Late and are Tired

If the enemy forces have already gained the upper hand by occupying an advantageous position, one should avoid engaging them. The troops that arrive late and rush into action are already tired and being pushed to fight, will surely be defeated.

Rule: One should occupy the battleground early to fight the exhausted enemy troops who arrive late.

Strategy 56 — Being Alert, not Complacent after a Victory

Strategy 57 — Being Prepared Despite a Victory

Do not be arrogant after winning a battle. Be on the alert always so that even when the enemy forces come, one is well-prepared to take them on.

Rule: Treat victory as if one has not achieved it.

Strategy 58 — Dealing with Defeat

Do not be dismayed if the enemy wins. Instead, look out for the good in an adverse situation, reorganise the weaponry, boost the troops' morale and wait for the enemy soldiers to become complacent to mount an offensive.

Rule: Consider the good in an unfavourable situation to avert further disasters.

Strategy 59 — Launching a Quick Attack

If one is sure of the possibility of winning over the enemy, quickly send soldiers to create disturbances among the enemy troops.

Rule: Launch an attack at the opportune time.

Strategy 60 — Withdrawing when Outnumbered

If one is outnumbered, the location is unfavourable and there is no way to engage the enemy, make a quick retreat to preserve the army.

Rule: In the face of a difficult situation, it is wise to retreat.

Volume 7

Strategy 61 — Fighting a Provocative Battle

When fighting a war, if the two opposing camps are far apart and the strength of both forces is about the same, horsemen may be deployed to launch an attack. Other troops can then lay an ambush. Should the enemy adopt this strategy, one should not mobilise the whole army.

Rule: To lure the enemy into making a rash advance, fight a provocative battle.

Strategy 62 – Gaining the Initiative to Fight

If the enemy is weak and one's forces are strong, one should lure them to come forward for battle.

Rule: Lure the enemy to fight but do not fall into their trap.

Strategy 63 — Fighting from Afar

Strategy 64 — Fighting from Near

Strategy 65 — Fighting Near a River

A water battle is fought at the river banks. One should take up a position at some distance from the river bank. In this way, the enemy may be lured into crossing the river without suspicion. If one is ready for battle, do not station troops too near the river.

Rule: Attack the enemy when they are halfway across the river.

Strategy 66 — Launching a Fire Attack

If the enemy troops are stationed near grasslands and their camp is made of thatched bamboo, make use of favourable wind conditions to launch a fire attack on them. This strategy is particularly useful during hot and dry weather conditions.

Rule: There must be a good reason for launching fire attacks.

1. Under what circumstances should we use fire to attack?
2. When the enemy forces are stationed on grasslands.
3. The enemy's camp is made of thatched bamboo and materials that are easily inflammable.
4. A good opportunity to use fire depends on where the enemy troops store their food and also when the weather is hot and dry.
5. During the Zhong Ping Period of the Eastern Han Dynasty, Han general Huang Fusong and the rebel Huang Jun troops were engaged in a fierce battle.
6. Huang Fusong was defeated and trapped in Changshe.

Strategy 67 — Besieging a City

Besieging a walled city is the worst strategy and should be adopted only when there is no other alternative. It takes at least three months to make shields and chariots; and to prepare weapons and tools. It takes another three months to build mounds for the attack. Soldiers will become impatient to fight and this will only result in heavy casualties. If the enemy's city walls are high with deep moats and where they have many soldiers but little food, with no external aid available, one can take advantage of this situation to fight a slow battle.

Rule: Fight a slow war only when necessary.

1. Forcing one's way into the enemy's fort is a strategy to be adopted only when there is no choice.

2. Preparations to attack a fort takes up a lot of time and energy.

3. Forcing oneself to attack without sufficient preparations will only increase the casualty rate.

4. Since the enemy forces insist on guarding their fort but has little food and no external aid, we should adopt the strategy of besieging them.

5. During the reign of Emperor Mu of the Eastern Jin Dynasty, Former Yan general, Murong Ke led an army to attack Guanggu city in Eastern Jin.

Strategy 68 — Fighting a Quick Battle

When surrounding cities, if the enemy side has few soldiers but plenty of food supply, and external aid, one should conduct a quick battle.

Rule: Attack the enemy forces which are few in number, but have abundant food supply and external aid.

Strategy 69 — Fighting a Well-prepared Enemy

When the enemy's formation is in good order and their soldiers are calm and stable, do not take on the enemy. Wait for changes in the enemy camp before attacking.

Rule: Do not engage a strong enemy whose banners are well-ordered.

Strategy 70 — Fighting a Confused Enemy

When the enemy's forces are not well deployed and their soldiers are confused, it is advantageous to attack them quickly.

Rule: When the enemy forces are in a state of confusion, seize the opportunity to attack them.

Volume 8

Strategy 71 — Division of One's Troops

When one outnumbers the enemy considerably, choose to fight in broad open plains to secure victory. If one's forces outnumber the enemy's by five times, deploy three-fifths of the troops as the main force, while the remaining two-fifths should launch surprise attacks on the enemy. If one's forces outnumber the enemy's by three times, use two-thirds of the troops as the main force and the rest for surprise attacks.

Rule: Divide the forces so that the battle may be conducted smoothly. Failure to divide one's forces when necessary will only create chaos within the troops.

If one is outnumbered, choose to fight in flat and wide plains.

The main force is responsible for head-on attacks while part of the troops should attack from another side.

During the Southern Dynasty, Chen Baxian led an elite force to suppress the rebellion at Houjin.

He divided the troops and surrounded the rebel army.

During the battle, Chen Baxian employed heavy archery units, stationed at the frontline, to fight the enemy. At the same time, horsemen followed from behind, thus securing victory.

Under certain circumstances, it is necessary to split up a large force. Otherwise, it will hinder the troops' movements and create chaos within the army.

Strategy 72 — Consolidating One's Forces in Battle

When faced with a strong attack from the enemy, consolidate one's forces to fight. Not combining one's forces when it's necessary only makes one vulnerable.

Rule: Dispersed troops will put one in a disadvantageous position.

Strategy 73 — Instilling Hatred Against the Enemy Within One's Troops

Inspire the soldiers' fighting spirit so that they will be full of fury against the enemy before the battle.

Rule: Soldiers can be motivated to fight through anger.

Strategy 74 — Boosting the Soldiers' Morale

Generals are able to fight because they are warriors; soldiers are able to fight because of courage. The morale of soldiers is boosted by war drums. However, this tactic cannot be used too frequently. Neither can it be used when one's troops are still far away from the enemy. In both instances, the soldiers' morale will flag.

Rule: When the soldiers' fighting spirit is strong, they should advance to fight the enemy.

Strategy 75 — Pursuing the Enemy

Investigate why enemy troops disperse without reason. If their banners are complete and and their drumbeats synchronised, with a central command; they may be retreating but are not defeated. If the reverse is true, one should go after them.

Rule: Never slacken one's vigilance towards the enemy. Be careful if they are retreating slowly.

Strategy 76 — Fighting a Retreating Enemy

When the enemy retreats without any reason during fighting, one has to find out why. If it is because of fatigue and shortage of food supply, deploy elite troops to pursue them. If they are returning after a victory, do not stop them.

Rule: Do not pursue enemy troops on their way back after a victory.

Strategy 77 — Taking the Initiative Not to Fight

If one is outnumbered by stronger enemy forces from afar and who have adequate food supply, it is wise not to fight them. Be on the defensive and wait for the situation in the enemy camp to worsen.

Rule: The initiative not to fight lies in one's hands.

Strategy 78 — Forcing the Defending Enemy to Fight

When sending troops deep into the enemy's territory and they refuse to fight to tire out one's troops, attack their leader and cause some disturbances in their camp. Cut off their escape route and food supply to force them to fight. Deploy elite soldiers to defeat them.

Rule: Despite the enemy's high walls and deep moats, one should attack their strategic areas which they will have to defend.

Strategy 79 — Avoid Engaging an Enemy with High Morale

When the enemy forces are strong, one should not fight them. Wait till they are tired out before attacking.

Rule: Avoid fighting an enemy with high morale and vigour. Attack them when they are fatigued.

Strategy 80 — Laying a Siege

When laying a siege, surround the enemy from four sides but leave an escape route for them. The enemy's confidence will be shaken and this will create an opportunity for one to attack.

Rule: When laying a siege, leave an escape route for the enemy.

Volume 9

Strategy 81 — Causing the Enemy to be Defenceless

To create noise in a battle means putting up an empty show of strength to confuse the enemy. By making a feint in the east and attacking in the west renders the enemy forces defenceless. They will not know where to put up defence. One can then attack the areas which are left unguarded.

Rule: One who is good in warfare causes the enemy to be defenceless.

1. The tactic of making a feint in the east and attacking in the west is effective in confusing the enemy.

2. This will cause the enemy to be at a loss, not knowing where to put up an effective defence. This creates an opportunity for one to annihilate them.

- The enemy forces are going to attack in the east.
- I predict it to be in the west.

3. This tactic allows one to manoeuvre the enemy according to one's plan and to achieve the aim of attacking them where they are least prepared.

- Oh dear! We've been tricked!

4. During the early years of the Eastern Han Dynasty, General Geng Yan made preparations to occupy Xian and Linzi.

- Although the city of Xian is small, they have a strong army and sufficient food supply.
- Although Linzi is a big city, their defence is weak.

5. He decided to attack Linzi but ordered his soldiers to spread the news that he would attack Xian.

- I'll conquer Xian in five days.

6. Geng Yan launched a sneak attack on Linzi. Xian's isolated defending army forsook the city and fled. Thus, the Han army was able to kill two birds with one stone.

A general who is good at attacking the enemy forces will try to confuse them, so that they do not know where to defend.

Strategy 82 — Using Peace Talks as a Means to Launch a Surprise Attack

Before fighting, despatch a messenger to negotiate for peace. The enemy will make a lot of promises but may not keep them. Select elite groops to attack them once they are complacent.

Rule: To seek peace without a treaty is a scheme.

Strategy 83 — Making Careful Observations of the Enemy instead of Fleeing

If one is outnumbered and surrounded by a large number of enemy troops, do not retreat in case of being attacked from behind. Form a circular formation with the soldiers faced outwards. If there is an escape route, block it to strengthen the soldiers' resolve to fight. Attack from all directions to achieve victory.

Rule: When outnumbered, consolidate one's forces to fight.

Strategy 84 — Being Cautious when the Enemy Forces Surrender

When the enemy forces come forward to surrender, find out whether it is genuine. Be far-sighted and make preparations – do not be lax in one's defence. Maintain strict discipline to ensure that the army is in good order.

Rule: To accept the enemy's surrender is similar to getting ready for an attack on them.

Strategy 86 — Maintaining Calm and Stability within One's Troops

A leader must be able to demystify myths of bad omen. During a war, when one comes across an owl perched on a banner-pole, or when wine turns red, the general has to clear his soldiers' doubts or fears. He can do so by ensuring that they abide by the principles of loyalty and obedience. Counter whatever is evil with the righteous, make use of the wise and able to correct the foolish who are superstitious.

Rule: Dispel superstitions and unwarranted suspicions so that one's soldiers will be clear of their objective and will not falter in the face of death.

Strategy 87 — Being Loyal to One's Troops in Times of Danger

A good general goes through thick and thin with the common people. He will not forsake his soldiers just to save himself and will persevere to the end with his subordinates.

Rule: In the face of danger, do not forsake one's soldiers.

Strategy 88 — Attacking the Area that is Easiest to Conquer

Always attack the place that is easiest to conquer first. If the enemy forces are stationed in several areas, one should attack the weak few and avoid engaging the strong enemy soldiers.

Rule: Those adept in warfare will gain victory in areas that are easily conquered.

Strategy 89 — Sowing Discord in the Enemy Camp

Look for opportunities to sow discord among the enemy leaders. When they have become suspicious of one another, deploy elite troops to attack them.

Rule: If there is internal unity within the enemy camp, try to disrupt it.

Strategy 90 — Using Baits to Entice the Enemy

Volume 10

Strategy 91 — Misleading the Enemy

Divert the enemy away from one's main line of attack by strewing thick grass with obstacles. Put up many banners to give the impression that one has many soldiers. When the enemy soldiers prepare to attack in the east, one should fight in the west. Put up a false front when retreating to prevent the enemy from pursuing.

Rule: Place obstacles in the thick grass to confuse the enemy.

Strategy 92 — Fighting a Fleeing Enemy

If one outnumbers the enemy forces, they will be fearful of one's strength. Do not be hasty in pursuing them.

Rule: Do not press an enemy in a difficult situation.

Strategy 93 — Taking Advantage of Wind Conditions in Battle

Take advantage of the favourable wind conditions to attack. When faced with an unfavourable wind condition, one can also make use of it to launch a surprise attack.

Rule: When the wind direction is favourable, take advantage of it to attack. If it is unfavourable, maintain one's formation and wait for the right time to do so.

Strategy 94 — Taking Advantage of a Snowy Condition to Launch an Attack

When there is continuous snow and rain, and the enemy forces are not well prepared, launch a sneak attack.

Rule: Strike at the enemy where they are least prepared.

Strategy 95 — Building up One's Forces for Battle

If one has been defeated before, there is a need to boost the troops' morale. Only when their morale is regained, then can they fight again.

Rule: Boost the troops' morale, allow them to conserve strength and regain energy.

Strategy 96 — Getting Rid of Cowardly Soldiers and Deserters, Calming Soldiers' Fears

Execute cowardly soldiers who may affect the morale of the rest of the troops. However, if the majority of them are afraid, one should calm their fears and urge them to fight for survival.

Rule: Get rid of cowardly soldiers and if necessary, teach the troops to make good use of their survival instincts.

Strategy 97 — Severing Communication Between One's Soldiers and their Families

When engaged in a war, sever all communication between one's soldiers and their families. This will prevent the soldiers from feeling afraid and homesick.

Rule: Cut off all communication links between soldiers and their kith and kin.

Strategy 98 — Being Flexible Enough to Adopt a Strategy According to the Situation

A good general must adopt strategies that are fluid enough to change in response to the circumstances.

Rule: To achieve victory, one has to adapt to the changed situation accordingly.

Strategy 99 — Fighting a Justifiable Battle

A war should be avoided at all costs and should only be waged as a last resort. A country should not engage in wars unnecessarily, as its resources will be depleted.

Rule: A country may be strong but continuous warfare will bring about its downfall.

Strategy 100 — Combat Readiness during Peacetime

A country should always maintain a state of combat readiness, even during peacetime. One's army must always be well-trained and prepared for war.

Rule: Be prepared for war even during peacetime.

A Brief Chronology of Chinese History

	夏 Xia Dynasty		About 2100 – 1600 BC
	商 Shang Dynasty		About 1600 – 1100 BC
周 Zhou Dynasty	西周 Western Zhou Dynasty		About 1100 – 771 BC
	東周 Eastern Zhou Dynasty		770 – 256 BC
	春秋 Spring and Autumn Period		770 – 476 BC
	戰國 Warring States		475 – 221 BC
	秦 Qin Dynasty		221 – 207 BC
漢 Han Dynasty	西漢 Western Han		206 BC – AD 24
	東漢 Eastern Han		25 – 220
三國 Three Kingdoms	魏 Wei		220 – 265
	蜀漢 Shu Han		221 – 263
	吳 Wu		222 – 280
	西晉 Western Jin Dynasty		265 – 316
	東晉 Eastern Jin Dynasty		317 – 420
南北朝 Northern and Southern Dynasties	南朝 Southern Dynasties	宋 Song	420 – 479
		齊 Qi	479 – 502
		梁 Liang	502 – 557
		陳 Chen	557 – 589
	北朝 Northern Dynasties	北魏 Northern Wei	386 – 534
		東魏 Eastern Wei	534 – 550
		北齊 Northern Qi	550 – 577
		西魏 Western Wei	535 – 556
		北周 Northern Zhou	557 – 581
	隋 Sui Dynasty		581 – 618
	唐 Tang Dynasty		618 – 907
五代 Five Dynasties	後梁 Later Liang		907 – 923
	後唐 Later Tang		923 – 936
	後晉 Later Jin		936 – 946
	後漢 Later Han		947 – 950
	後周 Later Zhou		951 – 960
宋 Song Dynasty	北宋 Northern Song Dynasty		960 – 1127
	南宋 Southern Song Dynasty		1127 – 1279
	遼 Liao Dynasty		916 – 1125
	金 Jin Dynasty		1115 – 1234
	元 Yuan Dynasty		1271 – 1368
	明 Ming Dynasty		1368 – 1644
	清 Qing Dynasty		1644 – 1911
	中華民國 Republic of China		1912 -- 1949
	中華人民共和國 People's Republic of China		1949 –

Strategy & Leadership Series by Wang Xuanming

Thirty-six Stratagems: Secret Art of War
Translated by Koh Kok Kiang (cartoons) &
Liu Yi (text of the stratagems)
 A Chinese military classic which emphasizes deceptive schemes to achieve military objectives. It has attracted the attention of military authorities and general readers alike.

Six Strategies for War: The Practice of Effective Leadership
Translated by Alan Chong
 A powerful book for rulers, administrators and leaders, it covers critical areas in management and warfare including: how to recruit talents and manage the state; how to beat the enemy and build an empire; how to lead wisely; and how to manoeuvre brilliantly.

Gems of Chinese Wisdom: Mastering the Art of Leadership
Translated by Leong Weng Kam
 Wise up with this delightful collection of tales and anecdotes on the wisdom of great men and women in Chinese history, including Confucius, Meng Changjun and Gou Jian.

Three Strategies of Huang Shi Gong: The Art of Government
Translated by Alan Chong
 Reputedly one of man's oldest monograph on military strategy, it unmasks the secrets behind brilliant military manoeuvres, clever deployment and control of subordinates, and effective government.

100 Strategies of War: Brilliant Tactics in Action
Translated by Yeo Ai Hoon
 The book captures the essence of extensive military knowledge and practice, and explores the use of psychology in warfare, the importance of building diplomatic relations with the enemy's neighbours, the use of espionage and reconnaissance, etc.

Asiapac Comic Series (by Tsai Chih Chung)

Art of War
Translated by Leong Weng Kam
   The Art of War provides a compact set of principles essential for victory in battles; applicable to military strategists, in business and human relationships.

Book of Zen
Translated by Koh Kok Kiang
   Zen makes the art of spontaneous living the prime concern of the human being. Tsai depicts Zen with unfettered versatility; his illustrations spans a period of more than 2,000 years.

Da Xue
Translated by Mary Ng En Tzu
   The second book in the Four Books of the Confucian Classics. It sets forth the higher principles of moral science and advocates that the cultivation of the person be the first thing attended to in the process of the pacification of kingdoms.

Fantasies of the Six Dynasties
Translated by Jenny Lim
   Tsai Chih Chung has creatively illustrated and annotated 19 bizarre tales of human encounters with supernatural beings which were compiled during the Six Dyansties (AD 220-589).

Lun Yu
Translated by Mary Ng En Tzu
   A collection of the discourses of Confucius, his disciples and others on various topics. Several bits of choice sayings have been illustrated for readers in this book.

New Account of World Tales
Translated by Alan Chong
   These 120 selected anecdotes tell the stories of emperors, princes, high officials, generals, courtiers, urbane monks and lettered gentry of a turbulent time. They afford a stark and amoral insight into human behaviour in its full spectrum of virtues and frailties and glimpses of brilliant Chinese witticisms, too.

Origins of Zen
Translated by Koh Kok Kiang
    Tsai in this book traces the origins and development of Zen in China with a light-hearted touch which is very much in keeping with the Zen spirit of absolute freedom and unbounded creativity.

Records of the Historian
Translated by Tang Nguok Kiong
    Adapted from Records of the Historian, one of the greatest historical work China has produced, Tsai has illustrated the life and characteristics of the Four Lords of the Warring Strates.

Roots of Wisdom
Translated by Koh Kok Kiang
    One of the gems of Chinese literature, whose advocacy of a steadfast nature and a life of simplicity, goodness, quiet joy and harmony with one's fellow beings and the world at large has great relevance in an age of rapid changes.

Sayings of Confucius
Translated by Goh Beng Choo
    This book features the life of Confucius, selected sayings from The Analects and some of his more prominent pupils. It captures the warm relationship between the sage and his disciples, and offers food for thought for the modern readers.

Sayings of Han Fei Zi
Translated by Alan Chong
    Tsai Chih Chung retold and interpreted the basic ideas of legalism, a classical political philosophy that advocates a draconian legal code, embodying a system of liberal reward and heavy penalty as the basis of government, in his unique style.

Sayings of Lao Zi
Translated by Koh Kok Kiang & Wong Lit Khiong
    The thoughts of Lao Zi, the founder of Taoism, are presented here in a light-hearted manner. It features the selected sayings from Dao De Jing.

Sayings of Lao Zi Book 2
Translated by Koh Kok Kiang
   In the second book, Tsai Chih Chung has tackled some of the more abstruse passages from the Dao De Jing which he has not included in the first volume of Sayings of Lao Zi.

Sayings of Lie Zi
Translated by Koh Kok Kiang
   A famous Taoist sage whose sayings deals with universal themes such as the joy of living, reconciliation with death, the limitations of human knowledge, the role of chance events.

Sayings of Mencius
Translated by Mary Ng En Tzu
   This book contains stories about the life of Mencius and various excerpts from "Mencius", one of the Four Books of the Confucian Classics, which contains the philosophy of Mencius.

Sayings of Zhuang Zi
Translated by Goh Beng Choo
   Zhuang Zi's non-conformist and often humorous views of life have been creatively illustrated and simply presented by Tsai Chih Chung in this book.

Sayings of Zhuang Zi Book 2
Translated by Koh Kok Kiang
   Zhuang Zi's book is valued for both its philosophical insights and as a work of great literary merit. Tsai's second book on Zhuang Zi shows maturity in his unique style.

Strange Tales of Liaozhai
Translated by Tang Nguok Kiong
   In this book, Tsai Chih Chung has creatively illustrated 12 stories from the Strange Tales of Liaozhai, an outstanding Chinese classic written by Pu Songling in the early Qing Dynasty.

Zhong Yong
Translated by Mary Ng En Tzu
   Zhong Yong, written by Zi Si, the grandson of Confucius, gives voice to the heart of the discipline of Confucius. Tsai has presented it in a most readable manner for the modern readers to explore with great delight.

Asiapac's Latest Title
100 Series Art Album

Forthcoming ...

100 Series Art Album

《亞太漫畫系列》

智謀叢畫

百戰奇法

編繪：王宣銘
翻譯：姚愛雲

亞太圖書有限公司出版